BY DEREK O'NEILL

Desire

For information about permission to reproduce excerpts from
this book write to:
Derek O'Neill
244 5th Avenue, Suite D-264
New York, NY 10001
E-Mail: info@derekoneill.com

ISBN: 978-1-936470-50-1
First Edition

Get a Grip Series © 2016
Editor: Nancy Moss
Front Cover Design: Derek O'Neill

DEDICATION

To all who read this book, I salute you for wanting to change the way you live for the better and for having the courage to be who you are as fully as possible.

To all who encourage me everyday to keep going and sharing their lives with me, family small and large. But most of all the little angels who came to teach me – Alexa and Blake, my grandchildren.

"Everybody hurts sometimes, and when we do it is nice to have Derek O'Neill around. His excellent little books on the things that get us, (fear, anger, depression, victimhood, mental blocks) allow us to find our way safely through our psychological minefields and arrive safely at the other side. Read them when you need them."

Paul Perry, Author of the
New York Times Bestseller
Evidence of the Afterlife

TABLE OF CONTENTS

AUTHOR'S PREFACE

Thank you for purchasing *Desire: Never Fulfilled but Grows.* This book has not come about as a result of my training as a therapist, but through some hard-earned lessons that I have experienced myself. This is how I know the path out of limiting beliefs and behaviors that hinder growth. The tools that I offer in this book have worked not only for me, but also for hundreds if not thousands of other people. I have shared these ideas and techniques in my workshops, one-on-one sessions, video and radio broadcasts, and on my website, and I have witnessed astounding results time and time again. Through observation of others, and myself, I have learned to identify the triggers and root causes of disharmony. Most of all, I have come to understand and apply the best methods for achieving peace and balance in life; not perfection, but real transformation and harmony that comes with learning who we are and what makes us tick. My 35 years of martial arts study has given me a refined sense of timing for when to strike with the sword to cut away old patterns, and when to use the brush to paint the picture of the life we deserve and can have.

The 'Get a Grip' series of books offers tangible, authentic wisdom that can help you in all aspects of your life. You've made a great choice by investing in this book. Enjoy the read, and take time to learn and apply the techniques. Let's change who we are together.

Derek

Desire

Never Fulfilled but Grows

UNDERSTANDING DESIRE – IS DESIRE RUNNING YOUR LIFE?

Desire can be defined as the longing for those things we feel we need or want, but where does it comes from, and where does it lead us? How is desire connected to suffering? How does your past, and your subconscious, play a role? Is the endless chase of empty desires running your life? How do we achieve higher, healthy desires, such as being happier and more loving towards others and ourselves?

If we trace back where desires come from, we find attachment and the fear that drives it. We are scared that we will not have love, or money, or status. We can even become attached to anger and resentment, sadness, or other emotions. Attachment exaggerates and distorts what we think we must have, and creates even more desire. More desire creates more attachments. It is a cycle that manifests into suffering. In order to break the pattern we must begin to learn how to let desires go. When there is less desire, there's less attachment and more room for growth and joy. Empty desire makes your world very small. Freeing yourself of desire expands every part of your life. It takes time and commitment, however, and a lot of patience.

If your goal is to have more happiness in your life, you must look at the role of desirous attachment. Are you gripped by the idea of that bigger house, higher paying job, or perfect partner? Are you on an endless chase to acquire things or situations that you think will bring you bliss or relief? Making a conscious effort to let go of these kinds of desires, and practice acceptance of the plans the universe has for us, can open doors to wonderful surprises and new energy. When we become aware of our desires, we interact with the world and begin to live with a higher level of consciousness and gratitude. You are creating your own life, all the time, by how you react to it and move through it. Desire, when it manifests as attachment, conceals your truth. Desire that drives your actions and emotions can shift the way you see the world and create a false reality.

We begin to form higher desires when we detach from expectation and move into acceptance of all – good, bad, and everything in-between. This is one of the most powerful elements available to us. We have to take back our power. We can create what we want but only when we bring our hearts, not just our heads, into daily life. It's from the heart that we can manifest our own true higher desires. Enlightenment is when even those higher desires drop away, but for now, reaching for a desire that promotes something virtuous will give you a greater sense of satisfaction.

Strong desires make it hard to be grateful for what you do have, right now. Even when it is not exactly what we would wish for ourselves, we need to say, "thank you depression," "thank you anxiety," and "thank you bank manager, who wouldn't give me the loan!" The more we say thank you, the more we eliminate the chances of it happening again and again. It is not easy to have gratitude for what feels negative or sometimes even traumatic. It must come in equal measure and with the same passion for everything that happens to you. This is a form of enlightenment. It is all part of your creation.

Before we dive into this exploration of desire, I want to acknowledge that desires that don't serve your higher purpose are not going to disappear from your life entirely. Just as it is important to welcome every element that comes to you, desire cannot be cut out of the whole of experience. Desire is a natural part of being human. Wanting something is not "wrong" or unnatural. It's how we recognize, explore, and process desire. There are many belief systems and teachings that incorporate a karmic view of desire, as something you are born into this lifetime with. The Hindus call it the garland of karma. You have a set of desires that were unfulfilled in a past life and because they were unfulfilled, you have come into this life again. If you have a desire to do something and it is a driving desire that will not harm others, you must fulfill it. If not, the karmic wheel will continue to bring you back here until you have that experience. If you repress a driving desire, it will only pop up again and again. It is one of the pearls on your chain.

Once you've gratified the kind of desire that kept you up at night, you usually find that it is not the answer, nor the path to true lasting happiness. It is the experience of filling a karmic, higher purpose that allows us to let go of the obsessive pursuit of the external things and circumstances that actually make a lot of people miserable. The suffering is in repeating the pattern, without gaining clarity and perspective. Buddhism uses the word 'tanha' or 'thirst' for desires that crave and cling to expectation and attachment. It's a lower desire that mirrors an addiction where satisfaction will never come, unless more is provided, in a never-ending chain of suffering. A good, higher desire aspires to and wishes for improvement and light, whether it be in service to others, better understanding, compassion or remembering your truth.

DESIRE AND ATTACHMENT – A CYCLE OF UNFULLFILMENT

Desire for possessions, money, or people can look like a solution to a problem or challenge in your life. We connect these external things to pleasure. We are attracted to pleasure, but once we get what we thought we wanted or needed, there is usually another desire that arises unforeseen in the infinite chase for what we think will satisfy us. If we are cold, we desire the pleasure of fire, but the dream can become a nightmare when there is so much fire that we need ice. Healthy desires (food, shelter, happiness, enlightenment) can be positive, unlike the pursuit of lower desires, yet we still have to identify what is genuine to ourselves in terms of what we really need.

So much of what your mind tells you is necessary is an illusion and driven by fear. When you base the definition of who you are on possessions, you will naturally fear loss of identity. When we start to see ourselves apart from the attachments we have formed, we can then find the freedom and joy of letting go of desires. It is a redefining that has to work against all the cultural messaging of our world that constantly tries to sell it. False goals fuel comparisons that only cause more suffering. It is an illusion that people buy into.

If we look at the concept of 'owning' in the bigger picture, the impermanence of everything is the only truth. Desiring to possess and cling on to something or someone is a misguided goal. We keep grabbing stuff we think we own. You think you own your house, but in a turn of events, the bank could own it. A career or job can end. A relationship can shift. You don't even truly own your life because you don't know when it will end and it can, at any moment. We've all watched the movies of people who just go around in life with a single backpack and they look so happy, don't they? Well, without making a drastic life choice such as that, you can shift your perspective and be attached to nothing. People who like to possess many things or feel the need to have a vast social network, actually have a lot of lack in their life. They collect objects and people to make them feel important because they don't believe in themselves.

One time I was on a fishing trip with a friend. We had put a boat in the water and then went back to the car to collect our gear. When we returned, the boat was gone. My friend said we should report the theft to the police. I answered that we had come there to fish and that we could rent a boat. At first he was confused at my response, but then he laughed and said that the boat must be insured because I was not upset to have it go missing. I told him that, in fact, I didn't have any insurance on it but we should just rent another. So that's what we ended up doing. I let go of the desire to own that boat. Perhaps someone else needed it more than I did. I thought, it's only a boat… I can rent another one. Life is much more peaceful when you start to think that way.

When you lose sight of what is truly important, your desires can cause a lot of pain and suffering. Pushing yourself to afford that big house or the expensive school for your kids – all to impress others – will bring you no joy. Many people are realizing that materialistic wealth is an illusion and a trap. We're starting to understand that any time we become attached to something and it's taken away, we will experience great suffering unless we redefine desire in our lives.

One of the best things that we can do is to consciously detach from 'things.' Resisting desire is especially challenging since there is a global culture of consumerism that admires and celebrates wealth, even when it is destructive to the larger common good. Some people are literally killing themselves to acquire more and more. Greed has worked its way into our society, so much so that at times we don't even recognize it for what it is. It's difficult to know what we can do to help fight against this tide. It begins with how you look at and process desire in your own life. It is only then that you can begin to help change the world around you for the better.

What does 'doing with less' mean to you? Is your sense of self-worth and security tied to things? If you had to give up many of your possessions, how would you feel? No one is suggesting that we can go from having a lot to a monastic existence. Start small. What can you let go of? Are you attached to the goals and objectives in your life, or are they aspirations that will truly fulfill you? What is your ego and what is your true self? Try to separate the two. During the course of your life, you are bound to lose a fair amount of what you have convinced yourself is necessary. You cannot control this. What you can control is your attachment to desire. Less baggage will make you lighter and it will be much easier to travel through your life. We all arrive here on this earth with nothing, and we leave it in the same state.

THE SUBCONSCIOUS LIFE OF DESIROUS ATTACHMENT

One of the most effective mindsets to be in for happiness, is to be free of desire. Though we need the basics of life – food and shelter – other needs, if we don't have the right attitude towards them, can lead to suffering. We have to learn to stop wanting unnecessary clutter in our lives. You must look into how your subconscious works and how attachments play a role. Fear, anger, insecurity, trauma, jealousy, and lack of self-worth are some of the many factors that can be the undercurrent of your mind's point of view. These must be acknowledged and let go. It is truly a matter of forming a relationship with your higher self in order to reach for higher desires. We need to understand that we are in so much abundance if we have food to eat and a roof over our heads. Our minds are also incredibly abundant in potential if we work on understanding our patterns of thought and begin to change the negativity.

You are creating everything by the way your mind works. When you transform your thoughts, your whole world changes instantly. Desire is not just manifesting the things people think they need, but it also is the way of thinking we become dependent on, even if unhealthy. The beliefs that you have about yourself are what will make the difference. Whatever you believe will be confirmed by your mind. If you believe that you are not good enough because of some external thing you do not have, your mind will agree. If you feed your mind positive affirmations about yourself, that is what it will become.

Often, your unconscious desires are stronger than your conscious ones because of attachments that run deep. We may have a conscious desire to be happier, or to be of more service, or to be wiser, but we get attached to a certain way of living. Whether it's the complaining about what you don't have, or perhaps the feeling that you don't deserve to live a better life, you are subconsciously attached to things and patterns of thought and behavior that are not serving you.

Happiness arises in the mind, not outside of yourself. A spiritual person, no matter what teachings or path they follow, understands this. They look within and to what has affected their view of themselves, and how they fit into the world. We can become very attached to ideas that we hold true but are not based in reality. What are the dynamics of your life story that may be shaping what you desire? How is the way you learned to deal with certain situations, perhaps just to survive emotionally, affected the desires you have formed over time? Can you trace feelings and beliefs that lead to empty desires, or to events that you are ready to examine and let go of?

The connection between subconscious anger and desire is something we rarely examine, but can reveal a lot about how we compensate for the hurt we think we can cure with external things. When anger arises, it offers us an opportunity to stop for a moment to ask ourselves, "What desires are not being fulfilled?" You can look back into your family, or something else from the past, where you felt you were not getting what you needed in order to feel secure. Your unconscious is controlling your world. The universe is not the master, you are! Whatever you are asking for, you are receiving. There's a voice inside your being that is stronger than your conscious voice, and it's manifesting your reality. When you ask the universe for something and it doesn't deliver, don't get angry. You will only give that unconscious voice even more power. That voice comes from all the pain, disappointments and jealousies you have experienced, from the moment you were born to where you are now.

When you look at the life you've led, and examine the root causes of your attitudes and actions, you will have the information to find your truth. Instead of blaming the world when you are having a hard time, stop and look inside. Take the energy of blame and shift it back into dealing with your own life.

LOVE VS. DESIRE

Love and desire seem to go together. We all know what it's like to desire to be with someone. As with any manifestation of desire, in love relationships we have to delineate between healthy desire and desire that is destructive, leading to suffering. Needing another person in order to feel complete or accepted is bound to lead to pain. The desire to truly share companionship and love can be diverted by unhealthy attachments. If we lack self-love and self-confidence, our desires sprout from a source that lacks stability and depth. We cannot get these qualities from anywhere or anyone but ourselves. Desiring that someone fulfill needs that can only come from within, is a recipe for heartache. The best relationships are free of desirous attachment, which breeds dependency, victimhood and narcissism. Attachment is about taking; love is about giving.

Whether you are already in a relationship, or you aspire to one, you must begin to examine desire and its role in the dynamic of love. Are your desires for another person healthy or more about what you feel is lacking within yourself? Take a few moments to think about or write down the things your desire in a relationship. What do you seek in the other person? How do you feel you 'need' them? Are those needs tipped in favor of being about you, or are they about the connection between you and the other person? Is your desire unselfish, or fueled by feelings of inadequacy, jealousy or competition? Have you made choices that compromise who you truly are? Sometimes desirous attachment is an attachment to desire! The chase of winning over another person becomes the driving force and love gets lost in the mix. Desire can only be part

19

of love when it is pure and serves your higher self. That is also what it means to truly love others.

Attachment is a hurdle to every kind of love – romantic love, family love, and love between friends. Boundaries are not clear when we are attached to expectations and outcomes. We ask more than people are capable of when we are attached to a desire for them to act in ways that we wish them to, or to say 'the right thing,' or fulfill our vision of 'the way it should be.' You cannot change another human being, and your desires must reflect that. Your attachments may be so deeply ingrained in your psyche that it's hard to separate out the delusion of expectation. In reality, we are not in control of the way anyone thinks, feels or acts. If we are responsible for ourselves, without blaming others, we can tap into a loving and virtuous role in all of our relationships.

Happiness doesn't lie in external people, places or things. It resides in our mind. If you chase after it, you are sure to never truly find it. When someone or something fails to 'make us happy', anger and resentment settles in. The suffering that springs from the desire to find 'the answer' in a relationship is bound to destroy connection and compound the feeling of isolation. When desire drives us, we are not grounded to our *own* identity and power. Desire exaggerates the importance of external elements, whereas love is acceptance of the realities of who we all are. When you love your partner or family member, you acknowledge and respect that they are their own unique, glorious, flawed person, for better or worse! Your choices about your relationships are best decided from a place of clarity. Desire can hide and disguise what is best for you.

TEACHINGS ON DESIRES

Many different spiritual paths and teachings include reflections on desire, and how it can keep us from our truth. Across the spectrum of thought, belief about higher desires – to do good and let go of lower desires – is a common thread. Being human means we experience desire. In order to live a spiritual existence, we have to look at desire and begin to define it differently for ourselves, and for the world.

The Bhagavad Gita is a Hindu spiritual text that comes from a larger volume of work called The Upanishads, which means 'to sit at the feet of the teacher.' The Bhagavad Gita includes important and insightful writings on desire.

There is a concept in the Bhagavad Gita that says, "Do not reach for the fruits of your actions." You are already on a royal road to happiness if you understand that happiness is the space between two pains, and pain is the space between two happinesses. With happiness comes pain. You must not be attached to outcomes. To be enlightened is to react in exactly the same way to both happiness and pain during the course of your life.

All that you perceive will disappear someday. Only consciousness survives. Everything you observe and feel is coming from your consciousness. When you go and smell a yellow rose, that yellow rose is not there for everybody on the planet. It is there for you alone, for you have created it with your consciousness. You have chosen to see a rose where others might choose to see a weed. Your consciousness is creating your reality. Take responsibility for what you are manifesting in your life and your consciousness will begin to create rose gardens upon rose gardens, all without thorns.

How do we connect with consciousness and learn to react with neutrality to all that arrives in our lives? The answer is very simple – you don't do it. It comes through you naturally when you sit in grace and become its vibration. If you chase after a result, the energy of desire pushes away what you are looking for. When you desire something very badly, you can be absolutely assured it's never going to arrive. There's a good chance you won't even know what you are calling forth with that desire.

There are four stages of meditation, or spiritual practice, that the Bhagavad Gita tells us we will move through, towards letting go of attachment and desire:

- The first stage of meditation comes with doubt and conjecture. You think "I can't do this. This is for other people. This is too big. I am too weak, etc."

- The second stage of meditation brings with it reasoning and pondering. You begin to explore and discover, opening your mind.

- The third stage of meditation brings joy, along with a sense of calmness and quiet. You stop reaching and sit in grace. You are just 'being.'

- The fourth stage brings a sense of omnipresence and expansion. You have become the bird singing to yourself, the tree that the bird rests upon, the food that it eats, and the air that it breathes. There is nothing that you are not.

Be still and be constant with your meditation practice and don't be hard on yourself. (A suggested meditation is given at the end of this book.) If you grasp for enlightenment, you will never attain it. The Bhagavad Gita tells you to just live your life and be happy. Listen to the birds! As you explore the Bhagavad Gita further, look into 'The Eightfold Path of Yoga,' which will expand your spiritual journey. The eight paths outlined are moral conduct, religious observance (the one religion of love), right posture, control of the breath, internalization of the mind, concentration, meditation and divine union.

By becoming more conscious of the way desire plays a role in our lives, we can surrender our attachments. The concept of 'putting a ceiling on desire' will help the process. The spiritual teacher Sathya Sai Baba spoke of it as an opportunity to curb the prison of desire that just multiplies, never satisfied, always wanting.

Desire is like the shadow caused by the morning sun; it gets longer when you run to catch it; it makes you a fool. - Sathya Sai Baba

Desire is the worst enemy; it ruins many a human life. Desire, when fulfilled, breeds further desire. - Sathya Sai Baba

Desire leads to ultimate ruin; it can never be destroyed by fulfillment. Dispel desire; develop true love. - Sathya Sai Baba

Sathya Sai Baba's teachings on 'putting a ceiling on desire' are also highlighted in a four-part program that speaks about: 1) how food is a powerful source of life that should not be wasted, 2) money must be used for good, 3) time is precious, it should be used consciously for positive efforts, and 4) that everything is energy. Desires that do not further love and service are a misuse of that energy.

Putting a ceiling on desires also offers you an opportunity to open doors to new ways of thinking and to finding joy. For instance, if you were used to staying in five-star hotels, and you can no longer afford to, it might be actually quite exciting for you to go to a hostel and spend some time there out of your comfort zone, a departure from the desires you usually fall back on. When we stop and readjust our desires to 'what we need' instead of 'what we want,' our systems and patterns begin to change. We get closer to our truth. Events and circumstances are always changing. Wherever you are at a certain point in time,is exactly where you're supposed to be in order to learn something.

In Buddhism, the teachings say that the root of all suffering in life is desire and craving. When we are attached to our desires, any satisfaction and happiness will not last, as we will continue to desire a never-ending chase of 'wanting.' Buddha spoke of these ideas and more in the Four Noble Truths, and offered The Eightfold Path, or Middle Way, as instruction for finding balance and mindfulness. When we are aware of how our attachments will cause suffering, we can begin to redefine them and let them go.

There is a wealth of thought, writings, teachings, and practices related to desire across many spiritual paths. I encourage you to explore the material and concepts mentioned briefly in this section, digging deeper and finding a transformative practice to integrate into your life.

ASPIRATION AND ACCEPTANCE – STOP CHASING DESIRE

Letting go of desire is easier when we look at the nature of those desires, and separate out what causes suffering. Is a particular desire about attachment to something, or does it aspire to a higher good? One could say it is impossible to reach a goal that is virtuous unless we are connected to an outcome. In reality, it is the process that we must embrace, and acceptance of whatever comes out of it. People who are perceived as 'driven' and 'relentless' are held in high regard in our culture, yet it is the people who understand how to move towards a goal without attachment that will find more happiness. Attachment is a craving of the ego. It distorts and confuses what is important. We become blinded by desirous attachment and suffer because of it. It feeds the ego to look for things outside of you. Inspiration and aspiration can be positive motivators. We have a choice about the path we take to attain something we want to accomplish.

Chasing desire is an empty exercise. No matter how much you take in, you will always be hungry again. It's not just the temporary satisfaction and need for more and more to get to that point, but also the inability to enjoy and celebrate where we are at this very moment. If you are always thinking that things would be better if you only had X, or that you would be blissful if only Y loved you, or that you would finally be respected if you got that job at Z, you are missing out on the here and now. You cannot be present if you are always chasing your desires. You won't be fully available to your situation now and the relationships that you have. Obviously there are changes we find that we would like to make in our lives, but if we focus only on a goal, and obsess about it, we are living half a life. When you are constantly on a chase, you are a ghost to the present, never content, and preoccupied with a future that you, in reality, have very little control over.

Understanding your desires and knowing what is truly important to you is where you will find happiness. If you have this at the start of any journey, wherever you end up will be fine. If you are waiting for the perfect scenario where the stars align in a flawless way for you, you will be waiting forever. Are you delaying your life? You may not even be aware how your desires can be making your world smaller and more painful. Are you always looking for what is wrong instead of what is right in your life? Are your desires really other people's desires that you have adopted for yourself?

Once you carefully examine the motivation and context for your desires, you can begin to practice shifting them and letting many of them go. Look at the chase as an opportunity to stop, listen to your heart, and begin to change the way your mind works. You have to dig deeper below the surface. When your desires lose their grip, you are free to experience more than you had ever thought possible. That is the great irony of desire. On the face of it, it seems like enthusiastic energy, but in reality it is a prison that makes your world more of a hamster wheel than a well-rounded life. Practicing acceptance, in a mindful loving way, opens a universe of possibility.

When we welcome all of our experiences with acceptance, we end the misguided pursuit for a particular result that we think we must have. If I were told I had just won a billion dollars in the lottery, I would say "thank you." When I heard "your house has burned to the ground," I would also say "thank you." As challenging as it may be to comprehend and embrace that attitude, it is a neutralizing, easy way of life. Wouldn't life be very boring if nothing went wrong? If you are alive, you are going to feel pain. Everything is a cycle, with no beginning and no end. We must accept desire. It will always be there but it can be reshaped and examined. How can desire become as positive of a factor in your life? Which desires can you hold onto without causing suffering? Desires will arise. It is what you choose to do with them that makes all the difference.

OUR DESIROUS WORLD

Between consumerism, conflict, and the 'noise' of technology, we can observe desires driving some of the least admirable ideas and behaviors. There's a false connection between money and happiness. Though this is nothing new, it has reached new heights and has seeped into our culture in a way that isn't even noticed. People are trying every remedy they can find outside of themselves to find bliss, when the answer lies within. All the things that people keep buying satisfy them less and less. The arguments and fights to 'win,' or prove that they are right, are empty battles if they don't feed the soul and further a loving, compassionate way of life. Technology that increasingly shapes our world is mostly an illusion and a hurdle to people having true human interaction. Young people especially desire to be 'liked,' 'followed,' and 're-tweeted,' as if that would be a true standard of value in who they are.

Love combats hate and anger. It is bigger and wiser than desire. A loving heart doesn't chase or distort or need desperately to be popular or admired. Desire distracts us from what is important. We lose sight of nature and humanity when desirous attachment takes first position in our lives. There's a gathering of awareness about ways in which some aspects of technology have driven us apart. And yet, there's still a disconnect about truly looking at the role of desire. We need to ask ourselves, both as individuals and as a society, what motivates us? Are we grounded in a value system that doesn't harm one another and the planet? Even if we work for a cause or speak out against something we oppose, do we understand how desire plays its role?

When we stop wanting something, we can enjoy it fully. Letting go of attachment, and allowing the balance of life to flow uninterrupted is how we tame and understand desire. Greed takes away from the natural equilibrium and corrupts. It can eat away at you and create divisions between people – on both a small and large scale. As mentioned before, one doesn't have to become a possession-less being, completely freed of desire. It's unrealistic, but when we do have desires, we get to exercise the choice of how we deal with them. Are you taking more than you are giving? Do you need as much as you think you do? Are you caring for the environment, the people in it, and yourself? Have you become dependent on devices, conveniences, and indulgences? How can you reconnect with love and detach from desire? Just understanding desire is the first, and monumental, step.

Uncontrolled desire can unintentionally destroy what is precious to us. We overuse it, want more of it, or think once we have it, we can do better. Desirous attachment is very much like addiction. Sometimes seeing a dramatic affect in your life, as we move away from chasing what we think we want or need, can bring great awareness and transformation. Letting go of attachments because they have become a matter of life and death is not necessarily the best way to grow and change, but experiencing the suffering that desire causes can help to open your eyes.

Technology and science have to take into consideration the natural world. Anything we possess or chase after has to be acknowledged as the elements of an external world we ultimately can't control. Society tends to define and categorize people. It is important to fight against identifying who you are by these illusions. Your identity springs from inside of you. Your mind might confuse, distract, and misguide you at times, but your heart is your truth. Connection takes work and care, along with letting go of expectations. There is no quick fix even though 'instant' results are constantly promoted. The path our lives take is full of unpredictable twists and turns. Technology and social media are wonderful tools but they need to be used with a conscious, mindful approach.

The mind creates a cycle of desire where 'if only,' 'if I had,' and 'if this were different' all lead to suffering. When we stop wanting, we receive. When we stop needing, we are provided for. One of the most important concepts, and one worth repeating, is that whatever is happening right now is meant to be happening right now. We are given what we are supposed to receive at any particular moment.

IMPERMANENCE – CHANGING DESIRE INTO UNDERSTANDING AND SERVICE

The true nature of life is impermanence. Change is inevitable, yet humans attach to people, places and things. They also attach to events and beliefs from the past, and wants and wishes for the future. Impermanence is the thing you can count on! If we are stuck in the past, we are overlooking that it's the past and we are in a state of change, even if we don't see it. If we are only focused on an idealized vision for our future, we are fooling ourselves into thinking we can stop events from possibly adjusting our path. Our desires must take into consideration the undercurrent of change we all live with. The thing or situation you are chasing after might not even be there once you catch it. Living in the future means you are not enjoying what you have now.

Once we accept impermanence, it is one of the easiest truths on the planet. We continue to suffer because we're ignorant of the fact that the nature of who we are is that of change. We grasp at the idea of security and expectation, wanting more and not having gratitude for who and where we are at this moment. We might see some beautiful lavender in a field, then come back in December to find it will look all ragged and disheveled. The reaction is to probably want to dig it up thinking it's dead. But it's not. It's just gone into preparation to come back again. I guarantee you, even if this lavender tries its hardest to come back as a rose, it's not! The flower knows exactly what it is. It's not trying to be a teapot, or a microwave oven. We are the fools who are supposed to be the higher intelligent beings, yet want to be everything except what we are - just beings. We want to entertain and amuse ourselves, we want the answer to everything, we want to analyze everything to death, we want to be happy, we want, we want, we want, and then we want some more. Stop wanting.

Regardless of what you desire, every event in your life happens for your enlightenment. Enjoy whatever is served to you and don't be so attracted to pleasure, because as soon as a little something goes wrong, it will be blown out of proportion. If you are attached to things and deny that you can lose them, your dreams could become your nightmares. The excitement of the chase, which you may think you thrive on, will not last. Everything is transitioning all the time. That includes your emotions. If you are depressed, this too will pass. Happiness comes and goes. All the money or other things that are perceived as 'security' will not change this. When you reach for higher, virtuous desires you will enter into a state of service and connection, which will bring you grace. Grace will bring you happiness, the happiness will bring you Divine delight, and Divine delight will bring you enlightenment in the life you are meant to have.

Desire seems to be about gratification and reward, but it is actually the embodiment of discontent and emptiness. It will never be satisfied because it is a moving target. Once at your goal, something else will replace it. Living in the present, letting go of attachments, and accepting impermanence are the answers. To want these is to understand what higher desires are. We, and everything around us, are part of a whole. If we grasp at the pieces we increase our suffering, and if we grasp at the idea that we never want to suffer, we will suffer all the more. In that way, the chase for happiness runs us right into the opposite.

What are some of the practical ways we can begin to let go of desires that do not serve us, or the world? Here are some suggestions:

- Bring mindfulness to desire. Stop when you have a thought that is driven by desire. Recognize the thought. Name what it is and allow yourself to have the feeling. Try to separate the desire from your identity and perception of self-worth. See it for what it is, and then let the thought go. This will help with obsessive thinking and skewed perception around desires.

- Notice the difference between a goal and an attachment. What are the choices we might have instead of being focused on only one result? What else could happen that would lend itself to growth and discovery as an alternative, if you can't have what you want.

- If you are in a relationship, think about the difference between love and desire.

Are you in love or only 'in desire?' Is your relationship about the two of you, or is it more about how you want to be seen by the world? Has desire exaggerated things – both good and bad – in the relationship?

· If you are looking to be in a relationship, is your desire to meet someone who is more about fulfilling your needs, or about sharing happiness with a partner and the willingness to experience the inevitable challenges?

Writing exercises:

· List the things you feel you need in your life.

· List the things you want. Go over each one and ask yourself how you believe it will change something you want to address. Think about the emotion behind the desire. Explore what you bring to the table in terms of your past that has shaped your desires.

- If there were things you received which you desired in your life, that turned out much differently than you first expected, write them down and acknowledge them.

- List what you feel are your higher desires. Then list the lower desires. What could you add to the first list? How can you begin to make changes to the second?

MEDITATION ON DESIRE

Meditation is a great tool towards learning to control our thoughts, and when desires arise, we have to use our mind to understand them and learn to let them go. Meditation can help you go deeper into who you really are, without the external elements we too often define ourselves by. The very process of a sitting meditation, where we must be physically still and quiet the mind, offers the opportunity to address desire (the desire to get up, to move, to think about what we are going to eat for dinner or how we are going to solve a problem), and put distracting thoughts away for the 10 or so minutes you meditate. Let go of goals, be kind to yourself, and allow your mind to settle down. A meditation practice will eventually rewire your brain.

Try to take some time out every day for meditation. Even quietly watching the flame of a candle for five minutes will increase your well-being. You will find the bliss and abundance flowing into your life, and a deeper understanding of your issues and problems. Just stop, close your eyes, take a few moments, offer a question, and then sit still. There is so much wisdom within you.

****

Make yourself as comfortable as you can. Take two or three deep breaths. As you exhale on the third breath, close your eyes, relax, and let go. While you are meditating, remember that nobody wants or expects anything from you at this moment. There is nothing for you to do except to relax. Allow your mind to settle into that space of peace. This is the time where you just switch off from the world.

Now imagine that above your head is a gold orb of bright light. It looks like the sun rising in the morning, or setting in the evening. I want you to feel the warmth of that sun. Imagine the gold orb is just resting gently on the top of your head. Then, see it going into your head, drifting gently and spreading warmth, resting your mind.

The gold orb now flows down from your head, into your neck, then into your throat, and begins to spread across your shoulders. It feels so warm and healing, as it eliminates your stress. The orb rolls down your shoulders and into your arms, gently caressing, healing, soothing and relaxing you. The warmth flows into your elbows, your forearms, wrists, hands and fingers. And then from your shoulders it begins to seep into your chest, eliminating any causes of stress that you may have picked up throughout today or in the past few days. Drifting down into your chest, into your abdomen, relaxing, caressing and caring for you. The gold light is like having an old friend return to you, filling the trunk of your body as it now reaches your hips. Again, feel the warmth of this healing gold light as it begins to flow from your hips into the top of your legs, from your legs down to your knees, you have all the time in the world. It cannot be rushed. It just gently flows at its own pace, a bit like watching honey drip off a spoon. Down your shins, your calves, into your ankles, into your feet and toes, and then going through your being into Mother Earth, carrying with it any fears, any anxieties, any hurts that you may have experienced in your life. Mother Earth is receiving all your hurts and just transforming them back into love and light.

As you just sit quietly, completely calm and completely relaxed, imagine that two angels have just come and are standing behind you. You may – or may not - feel them there but all that's important is that you know two guardian angels now stand behind you. If there are any issues going on in your life that you might need some help with, now is the time to ask these two guardian angels to help and guide you. Imagine that each of these angels begin to send gold light from their heart to your heart, taking away any sadness, fear, resentment, or disappointment you may have experienced in the last while. Feel these emotions lift, as if weight is being lifted up off of your being.

And now, as you're in this wise space of your own being, you begin to apply the teaching that says the best way to end trouble is to send love. If you can, at this time in your life, imagine the gold light coming from your heart to people, situations and experiences that you need to change now in your life. Let the gold light go from you to them. If you find it difficult to send this loving gold light, imagine the two angels are sending it for you on your behalf. Sending it to people who might have hurt you in the past; people who don't understand you.

We close the meditation by sending peace to all beings in this world so that they can experience happiness, connecting us all to learn from each other. When we come together, we gain deeper understanding than when we isolate ourselves. To work towards this goal is truly a higher desire.

****

They say that what you want the most you must give away, so the teaching goes. If you are looking for love, you must give love away. If you are looking for wealth, you must give wealth away. By giving it away, you energize the circle of light, and that circle of light will always return to its source. So what you give is what you receive. Always remember that when you sit in this type of quiet space, you will always be safe and secure. You will always be improving your health and well-being.

Every day that you quietly sit for a few moments, you will be increasing your well-being. You will be sitting in your own light, the power of your own creation, and the love of who you are.

ABOUT THE AUTHOR

For more than 20 years, Derek O'Neill has been transforming the lives of thousands of people around the world for the better. An internationally acclaimed transformational coach and therapist, motivational speaker, author, martial arts sensei and humanitarian, Derek inspires and uplifts people from all walks of life through his workshops, consultations, speaking engagements, media, and tireless humanitarian work.

Drawing on thirty years of training in martial arts, which earned him the level of Master Black Belt, coupled with his extraordinary intuitive abilities and expertise as a psychotherapist, Derek has pioneered a new psychology, transformational therapy. His signature process, aptly named "The Sword and the Brush," helps clients to seamlessly transmute their struggles into positive outcomes, using the sword to cut away old patterns and the brush to help paint the picture of the new life that they require.

In addition to reaching large audiences through workshops and media, Derek advises individuals, celebrities, business leaders, and politicians, helping them to find new perspectives on long-standing issues and bringing harmony back to their lives and businesses.

Author of More Truth Will Set You Free, the Get a Grip series of pocket books, a cutting edge book on parenting titled Calm Mama,

Happy Baby, and several children's books, Derek also hosted his own radio show, "The Way With Derek O'Neill," which enjoyed the most successful launch in VoiceAmerica's history, quickly garnering 100,000 listeners.

Derek is a master at offering practical wisdom and proven techniques for living a more harmonious and fulfilling life, bringing CEOs to the level of wise yogi and wise yogis to CEO; he has worked with executives from some of the world's major airlines, and the cast of Spiderman on Broadway to help transform group disharmony and untapped creative potential into productivity and dynamic performance. He has been featured in Exceptional People Magazine, The Irish Independent, The Irish Examiner, CBS television, and RTE, Ireland's national TV network.

Inspired by his worldly travels, he formed SQ Foundation, a not-for-profit organization focused on helping to solve global issues facing humanity today. In 2012, he was honored as Humanitarian of the Year and named International Celebrity Ambassador for Variety International the Children's Charity. He was welcomed as Vice President of the esteemed charity in May 2013.

Recordings of Derek's discourses are available for download, offering practical wisdom and proven techniques for living a more harmonious and fulfilling life.

To learn more about Derek O'Neill, to attend his next workshop, to order books, downloads or to contact him, please visit his website:

derekoneill.com

To learn more about SQ Foundation, the global charity that is changing the lives of hundreds of thousands of people around the world, go to:

sq-foundation.org

MORE RESOURCES FROM DEREK O'NEILL

Get a Grip Book Series
Abundance: Starts Right Now
Addiction: What a Cover-Up!
Anger: Who Gives a Shite?
Confidence: Easy For You to Say
Depression: What's that?
Desire: Never Fulfilled But Grows
Dreams: The Best Messengers
Excellence: You Never Lost It, You Forgot It
Fear: A Powerful Illusion
Forgiveness: So I Can Move On
Gratitude: Yes Please
Grief: Mind Boggling But Natural
Happiness: You Must Be Effin' Joking!
Mindfulness: Out Of Or In Your Mind?
Relationships: Would You Want to Date You?
Stress: Is Stress Stressing You Out?
Suicide: Fast or Slow
Weight: What's Eating You?

Other Books
More Truth Will Set You Free
Calm Mama, Happy Baby

Children's Books
Water Drop Coloring Book
The Adventures of Lucinda in Love-Filled Fairyland

SOCIAL MEDIA

YouTube
youtube.com/DerekONeill101
Facebook
facebook.com/DerekONeill101
Twitter
twitter.com/DerekONeill101
LinkedIn
linkedin.com/in/DerekONeill101